Original title:
Witty Woods

Copyright © 2025 Creative Arts Management OÜ
All rights reserved.

Author: Juliette Kensington
ISBN HARDBACK: 978-1-80567-427-6
ISBN PAPERBACK: 978-1-80567-726-0

The Glee of Greenery

In the shade of playful leaves,
Squirrels dance and weave with ease.
Frogs in ties and hats parade,
While whispers of the breeze cascade.

Mushrooms gossip with the breeze,
Tickling tales beneath the trees.
Laughter spreads as shadows play,
Cheerful moments chase gray away.

Fleeting Fables in Ferns

Beneath the ferns so lush and bright,
A rabbit juggles with delight.
Wise old owls share their views,
As chuckles echo in the blues.

Dance of critters fills the air,
With silly antics everywhere.
Storytellers weave their tales,
As mirthful laughter never fails.

The Satirical Spruce

In the shade of a spruce so tall,
Wisecracking branches jest and maul.
Pinecones tumble, making quips,
Home to wily woodland trips.

A raccoon dons a dapper suit,
Reciting verses, oh so cute!
Jests and gags fill every nook,
In this funny, leafy book.

Ticklish Twigs

Ticklish twigs with laughter sway,
As giggling breezes come to play.
Beetles wear their finest gear,
While humor blooms in every sphere.

A dance of shadows, light, and cheer,
Silly whispers fill the sphere.
The forest joins in playful fun,
Where every creature can outrun.

Romp in the Roots

Beneath the trees, we laugh and play,
With crooked branches pointing our way.
The squirrels chuckle, in secret they scheme,
As we trip and tumble, lost in a dream.

The sun shines bright on our joyous spree,
While we chase shadows, just you and me.
A toad hops by, wearing a crown,
And we can't help but giggle, falling down.

Punning Pines

Among the pines, the jokes abound,
Whispers of humor drift all around.
One tree cracks up, it quakes and sways,
While the other one says, it's just a phase.

A woodpecker pecks with comedic flair,
Tapping in rhythm, without a care.
We pine for laughter in this tall green maze,
Where jokes grow wild in a humorous haze.

Jocular Journeys through the Bramble

With tangled thorns and playful paths,
We dodge the bramble, avoiding the laughs.
A rabbit jests as it hops around,
While ticklish leaves join in the sound.

Berries giggle, ripe and bright,
Offering smiles in the golden light.
As we wander with glee, taking turns,
For each funny twist, our laughter burns.

Delights of the Dappled Path

On the dappled path, we skip and weave,
Where shadows dance, and we can't believe.
A fox in a hat tells tales of woe,
But the joke's on him, we all know!

Frogs in top hats refuting the sun,
As they leap and splash, oh what fun!
With every step, new laughter we find,
In nature's embrace, forever entwined.

Pranks of the Proud Poplar

In the breeze, the branches sway,
A poplar plots its grand display.
Leaves tickle a passing bird,
Chirps and flaps, a funny word.

Squirrels scamper, plan their spree,
Nuts concealed beneath the tree.
With a leap and an acorn toss,
The proud poplar laughs at the loss.

A shadow creeps, the scene is set,
Underneath, an unsuspecting pet.
With a rustle, the prank unfolds,
Bark giggles, as the tale is told.

In the twilight, whispers rise,
The proud poplar's clever guise.
Through the night, their laughter flows,
In the heart of green, the mischief grows.

Whispering Leaves of Laughter

Leaves whisper secrets to the breeze,
Giggling softly among the trees.
Branch to branch, the laughter spreads,
As shadows dance on grassy beds.

A rabbit hops, a hare agrees,
While rustling leaves stir merry tease.
A gentle push and down they go,
Falling leaves in a funny show.

A wise old owl perched above,
Cackles soft with a heart of love.
He hoots a tune, a chuckled rhyme,
As breezes make the moment sublime.

In the twilight, echoes blend,
Laughter lingers without end.
Beneath the boughs, we share a jest,
In nature's arms, we find our rest.

The Clever Canopy

Atop the hill, the branches grin,
Clever canopies begin to spin.
With fluttering wings, a joke is seen,
The tall trees scheme, a playful scene.

Across the way, a crow takes flight,
Dodging branches in the fading light.
Ripe for a trick, oh what a sight!
The clever canopy brings delight.

An acorn drops with perfect aim,
On passing creatures, it's a game.
With each plop, the laughter swells,
As echoes bounce within the shells.

As moonbeams kiss the laughter's sound,
The forest buzzes all around.
In the clever boughs where mischief glees,
We find our joy among the trees.

Jests Among the Trees

Under the boughs, the laughter roams,
Each trunk a host to witty gnomes.
They cast their jokes upon the air,
While critters giggle without a care.

A fox stands back, with a knowing grin,
Watching the antics, where to begin?
With a quick dash and a leap so spry,
He joins the fun as they all fly high.

The branches shake with every jest,
A symphony of giggles at their best.
Between the trunks, a playful race,
In this woodland, we find our place.

As dusk unfolds, the stars peek down,
Nature wears her jeweled crown.
With jests among the peaceful trees,
We dance and laugh, our hearts at ease.

Cheeky Cherries

In the orchard where jokes take flight,
Cherries giggle in morning light.
They play peek-a-boo in the breeze,
Making mischief with such ease.

Ripe and round, they bounce around,
With every plop a laughter sound.
They tease the squirrels, give them a chase,
In their vibrant red, no sweeter face.

A cherry tart spilled on the ground,
Sticky fingers and smiles abound.
Giggles echo, the sun starts to fade,
As cheeky fruits dance in the shade.

Quirky Quakers

In a cozy nook where plants all chime,
Ducks dabble in the rhythm of rhyme.
With bow ties and hats, a sight so bold,
They tell jests that never grow old.

They waddle with laughter, keep up the jest,
Each quack a punchline, they're truly the best.
Playing cards on a lily pad throne,
While the sun sneaks away, oh how they have grown!

Their dance is clumsy, a comical sight,
As they twirl and flail, what a delight!
The pond bubbles up with their cheerful flair,
Quirky quakers, beyond compare!

Riddles in the Rustling

Rustling shadows weave tales of fun,
Whispers giggle, a race to run.
Behind the leaves, a riddle is told,
With laughter that sparkles like jewels of gold.

A squirrel scratches his head in dismay,
As the breeze tosses riddles all around play.
"Why did the tree stop talking?" it sighed,
"Because it couldn't find its roots, it's tried!"

Every tickle of grass, a tease in disguise,
Each answered riddle brings a new surprise.
In the rustling, clever minds ensue,
A chorus of chuckles, a joyful crew.

The Gaggle of Green Gables

In the gables where greens always bloom,
A gaggle of giggles fills up the room.
Lettuce and cabbages having a spree,
Mischief abounds in this leafy jubilee!

The peas are peeking, making a fuss,
"Why don't we ever ride on a bus?"
The carrots chuckle, what a fine scene,
As they bounce and roll, oh they're so keen!

With every new pun, the garden will sway,
A parade of laughter brightens the day.
In their green kingdom, they reign so proud,
A gaggle of joy, always laughing loud.

Chuckles of the Cedars

In the shade of tall trees, a squirrel took flight,
With acorns as missiles, oh what a sight!
The laughter of pines, a rustling cheer,
As birds cracked jokes, their songs we could hear.

Under branches so wide, a fox made a joke,
While rabbits and deer shared giggles and smoke.
The breeze played along, with whispers of glee,
In this frolicsome grove, all nature was free.

With owls rolling eyes, and chipmunks so sly,
They plotted to prank every passerby.
The trees held their secrets, their own comic tales,
Of bark-biting beetles and antlered jails.

When twilight rolled in, the shadows did dance,
While shadows of laughter took their chance.
In the heart of the grove, smiles spread like a fire,
Forever we'll giggle, in nature's empire.

The Arboreal Antics

Beneath the tall oaks, the raccoons did play,
In masks and their antics, they brightened the day.
A turtle cracked wise with a slow-moving jest,
While the lizards laughed loud, inspired by the rest.

The trees bent to listen, their leaves all a-quake,
As wise old cypress shared tales that he'd make.
A bear danced a jig with a skip and a twirl,
And nearby a beaver critiqued with a whirl.

When dusk painted skies with colors so bold,
A crickets' chorus sang tales to be told.
The moon joined the fun, a spark in the glade,
Illuminating laughter, a sweet masquerade.

With every short breath, filled with warmth and cheer,
The forest preserved joy in each sapling near.
So gather your friends in this woodland delight,
For the antics are best when shared in the night.

Forests of Fables

Once in the woods, a porcupine sly,
Wove jokes with his quills that could make you cry.
A chorus of critters joined in with delight,
Each tale spun from branches, each chuckle took flight.

The cunning old crow, so crafty and smart,
Told tales of the deer who thought they could dart.
With antics so bold, and laughter so pure,
These fables of fun, in the woods would endure.

The sun peeked through leaves, casting warmth on the ground,
While laughter erupted from flora around.
Squirrels passed whispers on breezes so light,
As each critter shared jokes, a magical night.

So come leaf and limb to hear every yarn,
Of foxes and rabbits, and their charming charm.
In fables of forests, the humor won't cease,
With every tall tale infused with sweet peace.

Humor in the Hollow

In a hollow of wood, where the shadows all meet,
A gathering of laughter formed under the seat.
The insects were buzzing with stories so bright,
Of mishaps and blunders, all through the night.

A hedgehog tripped over his own little feet,
The frogs croaked in chorus, their rhythm was neat.
Each pun held a spark, each giggle a treat,
As laughter rang loud from the roots to the street.

With fireflies twinkling like stars in the gloom,
They flickered and danced, spreading joy like a plume.
Silly antics arose, no creature was shy,
In this merry hollow where spirits fly high.

As dawn broke the spell, the laughter remained,
A symphony sweet, in the landscape ingrained.
For humor's sweet breath lingers on in the trees,
In the heart of the hollow, where joy floats with ease.

Beneath the Boughs of Banter

In the shade where jokes take flight,
Squirrels conspire with sheer delight.
Leaves giggle in the softest breeze,
Even the acorns chuckle with ease.

Beneath the branches, laughter flows,
A place for quirks, where humor grows.
Twisted vines, in whispers share,
Secrets triggered by puns in the air.

Satire in Sylvan Shadows

In shadows deep, where critters scheme,
A chorus sings like a playful dream.
The owls wear glasses, giving advice,
As ants critique, oh, isn't it nice?

Trees sway gently with stories untold,
Echoing mischief that never gets old.
Frogs in tuxedos, oh what a sight,
Croaking humor beneath moonlight.

The Mischief of Moss

Mossy carpets plot and tease,
Tickling toes with playful ease.
Fairies breakdance, through soft green beds,
While giggling toads roll on their heads.

Whispers of moss in the twilight air,
Invite the fables of laughter to share.
Life in the underbrush, vibrant and bold,
Tales of whimsical wanderers unfold.

Grove of Grins

In a grove where smiles grow tall,
Woodpeckers drum a whimsical call.
Butterflies twirl in colors bright,
Dancing with joy from morning to night.

Gnarled branches twist in delight,
A swirl of laughter, a pure delight.
Every rustle, a giggle, a cheer,
Nature's punchline, loud and clear.

Smirks and Sycamores

In the shade of leafy greens,
Squirrels plan their schemes.
With acorns as their ballots,
They giggle in the beams.

Branches twist in playful arcs,
Whispers drift on breezy spark.
Frogs in suits with tiny ties,
Leap with laughter in the dark.

The sun it winks, the moon it grins,
Beneath the trees, the fun begins.
Nature's jesters dance around,
In this realm, joy doubles down.

So come and join this merry throng,
Where every leaf hums a funny song.
In the arms of green, we'll often find,
A silly heart and a playful mind.

The Laughing Larch

A larch that laughs with every breeze,
   Cracking jokes among the leaves.
  It sways and bends, a happy sight,
    Underneath the stars so bright.

Its bark is rough, yet full of charm,
   Whispering tales that disarm.
The creatures gather, drawn to cheer,
   Sharing stories, year by year.

With roots entwined in jest and fun,
Where moonlight dances, joy has begun.
  The shadows play a silly game,
While crickets sing a tune, quite tame.

A haven for the merry and wild,
  In this grove, they're nature's child.
Under the larch, the world feels right,
  Laughing together through the night.

Tittering Tumult of Trees

A rustle brings delightful glee,
As trunks conspire with secrecy.
Fluttering leaves, a giggling crowd,
Nature's jesters, merry and loud.

Beneath their boughs, the stories twine,
Echoing laughter, so divine.
With saplings sprouting punchlines bright,
And seasoned oaks with laughter's might.

The woodpecker drums a merry beat,
While hedgehogs tumble on their feet.
In this lively uproar of cheer,
Every whisper draws a giggle near.

So, let us prance and sway with ease,
Amidst the tittering tumult of trees.
In playful shades, we're free to roam,
In this forest, we all feel at home.

Jesting in the Junipers

In the junipers, wild and free,
Nature's jesters dance with glee.
Bending low with playful grace,
Sprigs of laughter fill the space.

The breeze it tickles, whispers cheer,
As creatures gather, drawing near.
With every rustle, every sound,
A cheeky grin can be found.

Tails a-wagging as they tease,
Among the branches, just like bees.
With every twist and turn in play,
The junipers brighten the day.

So join the fun, let laughter bloom,
Under the boughs, forget the gloom.
With playful hearts, we leave our cares,
Jesting in the junipers, no one stares.

Smiles in the Sylvan Silence

In a forest where laughter does spring,
Trees dance and sway, just like in a fling.
A squirrel in a hat, quite dapper and bold,
Tells tales of acorns, heartwarming and old.

The owls wear glasses, how smart they appear,
Reading the jokes that arrive each year.
Beneath the green canopy, giggles abound,
Nature is chuckling, what joy can be found!

Mushrooms are capers in a playful pose,
While rabbits in tuxedos strike funny prose.
The breeze carries snippets of whimsical cheer,
Even the sun seems to wink, oh my dear!

So wander through whispers where smiles bloom free,
Among silly shadows, pure glee is the key.
Nature's light-hearted, come join in the fun,
In the heart of this forest, our laughter's begun!

The Jestful Journey Through the Jungle

Swinging through trees, a monkey's delight,
Telling tall tales in the soft morning light.
With each vine he swings, he spins out a joke,
Leaves giggle along, joined in the poke.

Parrots paint pictures with words that they sing,
Quips woven brightly, oh what joy they bring!
An elephant trumpets a rhythmic old pun,
As creatures gather 'round, joining in the fun.

The snakes wear their smiles, all slithery slick,
Sharing sly humor, their best little trick.
Through thickets and thorns, let laughter ignite,
In this bustling bazaar of pure delight.

So journey along, where the giggles grow tall,
In the heart of the jungle, you'll find humor for all.
With every step forward, the laughter expands,
In the vibrant green life, we all give our hands!

Humor in the Heather

In the midst of heather, where daisies bloom wide,
Bumblebees buzz with a comical stride.
They tickle the flowers with whimsical glee,
Creating a concert, all playful and free.

A fox with a quip steals the show with a grin,
Rodents with riddles let the laughter begin.
The wind whispers jokes only daisies can hear,
As colors collide in a floral sphere.

Puffballs of dandelions float in the air,
Like tiny balloon animals, shiny and rare.
The sun's golden rays wink through petals and stems,
Crafting a canvas where joy never stems.

So wander through meadows, where smiles are found,
In a patchwork of echoes, let cheer abound.
With every sweet step, feel the humor's embrace,
In the heart of this garden, find laughter's grace!

The Chuckle of the Creek

By the babbling brook where the giggles emerge,
Water skips stones, as if it's a surge.
Frogs in their bow ties compete for the crown,
Croak out their punchlines, never a frown.

The fish flash their fins, like they're singing a tune,
As dragonflies dance, 'neath the light of the moon.
A turtle cracks jokes as he plods on his way,
Living his life in a carefree display.

The stones tell their tales, each ripple a jest,
Swirling with laughter, nature's own fest.
So wade through this waterscape, let your heart leap,
Find joy in each splash, in the depths, laughter steep.

In the chuckle of currents, life's humor runs deep,
Follow the trail of smiles, don't you dare sleep!
Join the merry crew where the fun never ends,
At the edge of the creek, where laughter transcends!

Whimsy Amongst the Willows

Beneath the branches, tales unwind,
Squirrels plotting mischief, oh so kind.
Twirling leaves like dancers on the floor,
Breezes giggle, always wanting more.

A rabbit wears a tie, quite dapper,
While frogs croon ballads in a caper.
The sun peeks through a leafy veil,
Casting shadows where giggles sail.

Ducks don hats and share a toast,
A quirky party, we love the most.
Chasing fireflies in the dusk,
Each glow a treasure, a whimsical musk.

So join the fun, don't you delay,
In this lively grove, we laugh and play.
With every rustle, a chuckle's near,
Nature's humor, always clear.

Fables of the Frisky Ferns

In the shade where shadows tease,
Ferns plot pranks with effortless ease.
A snail in a sweater, what a sight,
Attempting to dance in the pale moonlight.

Caterpillars gossip on the vine,
Trading tales over cups of brine.
The grasshoppers leap with flair so grand,
Making wild music across the land.

Twilight catches critters in jest,
Chasing moonbeams, they never rest.
Each rustle's a laugh, a cheerful sound,
In this forest where joy abounds.

The wind joins in, a playful tune,
Tickling the trees beneath the moon.
With every giggle, the night unfolds,
A world of wonder, where laughter molds.

The Antics of the Aged Oaks

Ancient oaks with stories vast,
Whisper jokes from the distant past.
Their branches sway with winks and grins,
Sharing secrets where laughter begins.

Squirrels wear shoes, oh what a sight!
Fumbling their steps in the soft moonlight.
A family of raccoons softly croon,
Harmonizing under the cheeky moon.

The acorns tumble like giggling friends,
Finding new paths as the day bends.
A committee of bees debates the best,
And honey's voted the ultimate jest.

As shadows deepen, the nighttime thrives,
Quirky creatures lead their vibrant lives.
In this sanctuary, smiles abound,
Where every rustle sings a joyful sound.

Lighthearted Lullabies of the Land

When dusk paints colors across the sky,
Crickets serenade, their sweet lullaby.
A hedgehog trundles, in curious gait,
Searching for friends, it can hardly wait.

Fireflies twinkle like stars on the ground,
Every flicker an invitation found.
Mice trade secrets, all giggles and cheer,
Sharing stories of mischief without any fear.

The moon chuckles softly, casting her glow,
While shadows of butterflies dance to and fro.
The world spins round under starry delight,
With whimsy and laughter guiding the night.

So hush, dear friend, let dreams take their flight,
Embrace the enchantment of this playful night.
In nature's embrace, perhaps you will see,
Life's little wonders, wild and carefree.

The Clever Chirp of the Sparrows

In a tree so tall and wide,
Chirps and twitters can't abide.
Sparrows leap and flap with glee,
Their songs echo, wild and free.

A sneaky crow glances around,
Hoping to snatch a crumb from the ground.
With a wink, the sparrows plot,
A joke or two, they catch the spot.

From twig to twig, they flit and fly,
Telling tales that make you cry.
The funniest stories they share,
With every chirp, they fill the air.

When evening falls, the laughter soars,
Underneath the leafy floors.
In the hush, a last chirp rings,
What joy the clever sparrow brings!

Capers in the Canopy

Up above where branches sway,
Monkeys leap and dance all day.
They toss bananas as they grin,
Climbing high with silly spin.

Squirrel joins with a cheeky tail,
Chasing shadows without fail.
Through the leaves, they scurry fast,
With every turn, a giggle cast.

A parrot squawks with vibrant flair,
Telling jokes that fill the air.
Each pun and jest, a playful tease,
Laughter floats upon the breeze.

As twilight whispers through the trees,
The canopy still hums with ease.
In this world of leafy fun,
The capers stall, but never done!

The Trickster's Trail

Down the path where shadows play,
A fox claims victory today.
With a grin and a flick of his tail,
He leads friends on a comical trail.

Rabbits hop, and hedgehogs roll,
Chasing laughter, that's their goal.
Every twist hides a funny scene,
Like falling leaves, they tumble, keen.

The trees whisper secrets they know,
While squirrels chatter, moving slow.
It's a riddle wrapped in a jest,
On the trickster's trail, they feel their best.

As the sun sets, shadows play,
The woodland laughs at the end of the day.
With every step, a new surprise,
The trickster's charm never dies.

Jingle of the Jolly Juniper

Beneath the boughs of juniper sweet,
Dancing critters keep the beat.
With tiny paws and merry hops,
Every moment, happiness pops.

Birds in bowties sing in tune,
A moonlit ball, beneath the moon.
They swing from branches, clapping paws,
The jingle rings, it's without flaws!

Raccoons with hats and bows so bright,
Juggle berries, what a sight!
Laughter flows like bubbles from springs,
In the juniper, joy sings.

As night descends, the fun won't cease,
In this grove, they find their peace.
Each little jingle, a chance to play,
In the merry heart of the woodland fray!

Sly Squirrels and Snickering Streams

Squirrels scamper with endless glee,
Chasing their tails, wild and free.
Streams chuckle, ripple, and play,
Nature's jesters, brightening the day.

Rabbits hop, with twitches and twirls,
While peeking shyly, oh what whirls!
Foxes grin with a glint in their eyes,
Crafting mischief beneath sunny skies.

The breeze carries laughter so light,
As shadows dance, a comical sight.
Each rustle and giggle, a joyful sound,
In this playful realm where smiles abound.

Giggling Glades

In glades where giggles echo wide,
Little ones play, their joy can't hide.
Trees sway gently, like they're in on a joke,
A chorus of laughter from every oak.

Chipmunks chatter with a cheeky flair,
Stumbling over roots without a care.
Breezes whisper secrets, just for fun,
The glades are alive, with joy on the run.

Sunlight dapples with a twinkling tone,
Shadows stretch out like a playful loan.
Nature's in on it, with a wink and a nod,
In these giggling glades, we're awfully flawed.

A Jest in the Juniper

Underneath the juniper, a trickster waits,
With a cap full of giggles and curious traits.
The air is thick with mischievous cheer,
As whispers of laughter drift near.

Beneath the branches, a dance unfolds,
With fawns frolicking in stories untold.
Dancing shadows tease the sun's bright gaze,
In the juniper's shade, hearts set ablaze.

Mice skitter, adding to the play,
With snippets of jokes that brighten the day.
The wise old owl gives a chuckle or two,
Holding secrets of comedy, tried and true.

Mirth Under the Maple

Beneath the maple, where laughter spills,
Sunbeams tickle, creating joyful thrills.
With roots that wiggle and branches that sway,
It's a riot of fun in nature's ballet.

The songs of the birds are nonsensical tunes,
Harmonizing with the bright afternoon moons.
Frogs croak rhythms, they just can't resist,
In this zany ecosystem, a humorous twist.

Squirrels plan parties with acorns galore,
While critters gossip and chatter and roar.
In this vibrant symphony of playful delight,
Mirth under the maple, oh what a sight!

Frolics of the Forest Floor

Squirrels chatter, nuts in tow,
Dancing leaves, putting on a show.
Mushrooms giggle, tiny hats,
While rabbits pull their prancing acts.

Breezy tickles, the ferns they sway,
A dance-off starts, hip-hip hooray!
Acorns cheer, with booming sound,
As critters frolic, joy unbound.

Fluffy clouds with faces grin,
As nature spins, the fun begins.
A butterfly in shades of blue,
Winks at a beetle, watching too.

From dawn to dusk, the laughter flows,
In this realm where silliness grows.
With every twist, a new surprise,
Nature's jesters, oh what a rise!

The Sage and the Spruce

In a cozy nook where secrets dwell,
A wise old sage begins to tell.
With spruce so tall, it quirkily leans,
Rooted in laughter, bursting at the seams.

"Why did the tree cross the way?" he mused,
"To leaf the chatter, for a snooze!"
The spruce barked back with a chuckling sound,
"Prickly one-liners, joy is found!"

Together they spun tales of cheer,
With branches waving, all could hear.
"Knock, knock!" said one, "Who's there?"
"Pine!" they cried, with giggles to share.

As dusk painted skies in hues of jest,
The sage and spruce felt truly blessed.
In their wise and witty talk,
The forest danced, with every walk.

Sassy Shadows at Sundown

When daylight slips, and shadows play,
The forest comes alive at the end of the day.
"Who turned out the lights?" a fox called sly,
"Let's throw a party, oh my, oh my!"

The owls hoot, with grins so wide,
While fireflies twinkle like stars at their side.
With every wink, the dusk grows bold,
As whispers of laughter begin to unfold.

Mischievous shades dance with delight,
A raccoon steals snacks in the soft twilight.
"Best of luck," says the brash little hare,
"Catch us if you can, if you dare!"

A jig in the dark, they leap and bound,
In the sassy shadows, true joy is found.
With every giggle, the night takes flight,
In this playful realm of pure delight.

Riddles in the Roots

Deep in the soil where riddles grow,
A wise old tortoise lays low.
"What walks on four legs in the morn,
On two at noon, and three when worn?"

The roots chuckle, their fibers weave,
Stories of antics, who would believe?
"Just ask the crow, she knows it best!"
The tortoise smirks, a riddle quest.

"Why did the worm refuse to dance?"
"Because he lost his chance in romance!"
Laughter bubbles through leafy spouts,
In the whispers of nature, joy never doubts.

As moonlight casts its silver glow,
The forest hums with the wisdom they sow.
From riddles shared to chuckles bright,
These playful roots bring pure delight.

Whispers of the Clever Grove

In a glen where giggles flow,
Squirrel in a bow tie, putting on a show.
A wise old owl with a wink so sly,
Counts the stars as they drift by.

Mice in sneakers race for fun,
Chasing shadows, on the run.
Breezes carry chuckles light,
As fireflies dance to the moon's delight.

Trees wear hats made of green,
Hosting a party, often unseen.
Laughter echoes, a joyful tune,
Beneath the watchful silver moon.

With every rustle, tales unfurl,
Of antelope who danced and twirled.
Here in the grove, mishap turns bright,
With each prank, comes pure delight.

The Quirky Canopy

Above, the branches twist and play,
Chatty leaves gossip all day.
A raccoon in overalls snickers so,
While clever vines put on a show.

One cheeky branch sways and dips,
As squirrels balance on sunshine trips.
The sun peeks through, a spotlight beam,
On all the critters chasing a dream.

A snail in a hat joins the parade,
With a punchline that never does fade.
Every nook hides laughter's echo,
As nature's humor begins to flow.

In this canopy, oddities abound,
Where every sound spins humor around.
It's the place where we all can be,
Full of whimsy, wild, and free.

Laughter Among the Leaves

The branches chatter in bright delight,
As the sun fades into the night.
A chameleon plays peek-a-boo,
Changing colors for each giggle anew.

The raccoons hold a pancake feast,
With syrup dribbles from the least.
Owls hoot jokes, sharp and witty,
In this green enclave, oh so pretty.

A mockingbird sings tales of cheer,
Of playful pranks that draw us near.
Breezes bring whispers of jest,
Nature's playground, never at rest.

With each leaf that twirls and spins,
Echoes of laughter drown out the winds.
The trees listen as we share,
In this laughter-filled, magical air.

Chronicles of the Playful Pines

In the heart of the pines, mischief stirs,
Beneath the boughs, there's a world of blurs.
A hedgehog in glasses writes it all down,
While a deer with a crown twirls around.

Chipmunks in tuxedos dance on ground,
As a funny frog hops around.
Raccoons juggle acorns, round and sly,
With a wink to the moon up high.

In a nook, a turtle tells tall tales,
Of treasure hunts and ship sails.
Giggles burst like bubbles in the breeze,
As playful creatures aim to please.

Chirps and chortles fill the air,
In this playful realm beyond compare.
The chronicles grow with every laugh,
A tapestry woven on nature's path.

Tree Talk and Tales

Leaves whisper secrets and giggle,
Branches sway like they're in a wiggle.
Roots joke about how they're stuck down,
While squirrels debate who's the funniest clown.

A bird sings of mates who are lost,
While mushrooms mingle, no matter the cost.
The wind tells tales of a silly kite,
That tangled with branches in a playful fight.

The owl hoots riddles all night long,
While raccoons gather to sing silly songs.
Beneath starry skies, the trees sway and sway,
In the woods where laughter finds its way.

A twig trips a fox on its merry dash,
As shadows waltz in a whimsical flash.
In this enchanted, giggly domain,
Nature's humor drives away the mundane.

A Quirky Quest in the Wilderness

In the thicket where oddities roam,
A turtle dons a top hat, far from home.
A bear with a bowtie struts with grace,
While a rabbit's got hiccups, it's just a phase.

Through tangled vines, a raccoon breaks dance,
Spinning and twirling, it's all by chance.
A gopher with glasses reads the trees,
Telling tall tales of the swaying leaves.

A porcupine juggles acorns with ease,
While owls throw shade on the summer breeze.
They chuckle and hoot at a squirrel's grand quest,
To find the best nut—he'll never rest.

As shadows stretch long in the setting sun,
The laughter and antics have just begun.
Each critter a character, funny and sweet,
In nature's playground, they shimmy and greet.

The Humor of the Hollow

Deep in the hollow where shadows play,
The trees share stories in a comical way.
A grumpy old turtle with wise, rolling eyes,
Jests about life's hilarious, silly ties.

A hedgehog in tails sings a tuneful rhyme,
About mishaps that happen all the time.
Nearby, a fox with a sneaky smile,
Plots pranks and schemes that stretch a mile.

The moon chuckles softly, so round and bright,
As fireflies boogie, dancing with delight.
Their glow lights the laughter, a twinkly sight,
In a hollow where jokes soar high like a kite.

With each sound of rustling, a giggle escapes,
From bushes where bushy-tailed antics take shapes.
So come join the fun, let whimsy unfold,
In the hollow where humor's a treasure to hold.

Revelry in the Rainforest

In the rainforest's depths, where verdant vines cling,
Came a parrot who danced and made voices sing.
With feathers so bright, it mimicked the frogs,
While monkeys played pranks, hiding in logs.

A chameleon chuckled, changing its hue,
As it tried to blend in, but who knew it was blue?
The sloths rolled their eyes, slow-motion jest,
While a jaguar laughed, dressed in a festive vest.

Under a sky where the sun's not alone,
A festival blooms of laughter and tone.
Each creature partakes in this joyous parade,
Nature's own revelry, a vibrant charade.

So when raindrops come dancing upon the leaves,
The jokes and the chuckles spin tales like weaves.
In this lush, lively haven, let spirits soar high,
For humor's a treasure that sweetens the sky.

Jolly Walks Through the Wilderness

In the realm where the trees wear shoes,
Squirrels discuss their latest muse.
With branches swaying and leaves that dance,
Nature beckons all for a funny prance.

The sun peeks through with a soft, warm grin,
Birds whistle tunes, let the laughter begin.
A rabbit in shades struts with flair,
While a deer plays tunes on a woodland chair.

Beneath the twist of the vines so grand,
A fox tells tales, all unplanned.
The flowers giggle, swaying about,
In this merry place, there's never a doubt.

Oh, the giggles and chuckles echo clear,
As critters gather, spreading cheer.
Join the jolly parade, don't be shy,
In this land of laughter, come up and fly!

The Laughing Labyrinth

In a maze of trees, where shadows romp,
Each twist and turn leads to a chomp.
The hedgehogs chuckle, the owls wink,
As paths intertwine, we stop to think.

Round every corner, a quip awaits,
From the cats who play with fate.
A jester frog leaps with a jig,
While gnomes debate in a tiny gig.

Flowers wear crowns of colorful hue,
Whispering secrets only to you.
With each step taken, a smile spreads,
In this puzzling land, where whimsy treads.

Lay down your worries, enter the fun,
The labyrinth laughs, it has just begun.
With giggles and glee, it beckons all,
To dance through the maze and answer the call!

Glimmering Giggles Beneath the Green

Under the boughs where shadows play,
Laughter sparkles like the sun's ray.
A dance of fireflies twinkles bright,
As critters converse in the soft moonlight.

Moss-covered stones sport silly hats,
Where raccoons plan their midnight chats.
With every rustle, there's laughter found,
Beneath the green, joy knows no bound.

Chasing shadows and singing songs,
Here, even trees join in with throngs.
A rollercoaster of chuckles and spins,
Where the world is bright and no one sins.

So gather around, join the fun spree,
In this glimmering realm, wild and free.
With giggles concealed beneath each leaf,
Let's revel together, what a relief!

Mischievous Mushrooms

In the damp of the woods, with caps so round,
Mushrooms whisper, plotting mischief profound.
They giggle and wiggle in the soft, wet ground,
As the toadstools chuckle, their secrets unbound.

They boast of tales from the damp, dark night,
Of adventurers lost, with a giggle of fright.
In their polka dots, they strut with cheer,
As the shadows sway and invite us near.

With a sprinkle of dust from a sprite's old shoe,
They dance in a circle, just me and you.
Around the trunk, they hop, they swoop,
Inviting all creatures to join in the loop.

So if you wander where the wild things hide,
Listen closely and let your heart decide.
Join the merry band, let laughter bloom,
In the world of mischief beneath the mushroom!

Playful Pines

In the grove where laughter sways,
Trees wear smiles on sunny days.
With branches bent in silly poses,
They play charades with the roses.

The whispers dance among the leaves,
As pinecones plot and tease with ease.
A squirrel jokes and leaps on high,
While birdies chirp a lullaby.

Roots entwined like friends so dear,
They share their jokes, not one a fear.
With every rustle, giggles sway,
The forest boasts a grand display.

So join the fun, take flight and spin,
In playful pines where grins begin.

The Quip Tree

Once there stood a tree so grand,
With a knack for jest, and jokes well planned.
Its bark told tales, both wise and spry,
As breezes carried laughter by.

Leaves would rumble, chuckles loud,
As critters gathered, forming a crowd.
The acorns burst with clever lines,
Such humor hid within the pines.

The trunk would crack a smile or two,
While branches waved their witty cue.
In every ring, a tale was spun,
A legacy of joy and fun.

So if you seek a dose of cheer,
Visit the tree, it's always near.

Sassy Saplings

Young saplings strut with playful flair,
With curly leaves and mischief rare.
They gossip softly, sharing glee,
In every breeze, their chortles flee.

Rooted deep but spirits high,
They dance about, they twirl and fly.
With each soft creak, a witty tease,
They joke with frogs and buzzing bees.

The sun spills light on their cheeky dance,
While shadows loom, they take their chance.
A playful wink, a dandy wave,
In every breeze, their humor's brave.

So chuckle with them, young and spry,
In playful groves where laughter's nigh.

Joking in the Jungle

Deep in the thicket where shadows grow,
Loud capers echo, they steal the show.
With monkeys swinging, tales abound,
As laughter ricochets all around.

The vines entwine in a tangled jest,
While parrots squawk, they leave no rest.
A lion grins with a toothy smile,
In the heart of jokes, he stays awhile.

The creatures gather to share their pranks,
With cheeky chimes and playful ranks.
The jungle sings a song of glee,
A rollicking buzz, wild and free.

So come take part in this laughing spree,
Where every bush holds a joke, you see.

Breezy Banter of the Boughs

In the trees, the gossip flows,
Squirrels chuckle at the crows.
Rabbits hop with jokes to share,
While the branches dance in air.

A woodpecker's tap, a clever jest,
The forest's chatter, a vibrant fest.
Leaves giggle as they twist and twirl,
Nature's humor, a flag unfurl.

Sunbeams laugh, casting silly sights,
Acorns roll like playful knights.
In each nook, a quip's concealed,
Among the trees, joy's revealed.

The breeze hums tunes of cheerful cheer,
Echoing laughter, loud and clear.
In this lively woodland spree,
Every tree's a comedy!

Follies of the Fern Fronds

Fern fronds waving with such flair,
Whispers rise like scents of air.
Joking shadows play on ground,
In this place, smiles abound.

A lizard slips, a comical sight,
While chattering insects take flight.
Each droplet of dew, a splash of glee,
Nature's jesters, wild and free.

With every rustle, a story unfolds,
Of bearded moss and ancient holds.
Dancing fungi in little shoes,
The punchlines change, just like views.

In the tangled greens, humor thrives,
Silly antics, laughter drives.
Beneath the ferns, join the fun,
In this jest, we all are one!

The Peculiar Pathway

Along the track, where shadows play,
Pebbles giggle, leading the way.
Twists and turns, oh what a ride,
This quirky trail can't be denied.

A hedgehog winks, a mousy prank,
As all the flowers brightly clank.
Misplaced signs that laugh and tease,
Inviting travelers with such ease.

With every step, a chuckle grows,
Underfoot, the mischief flows.
The path is winding, turns with flair,
Nature's humor fills the air.

Join the fun on this odd route,
Where each surprise is a hoot!
In this merry little chase,
Find your joy at every pace.

Chortles in the Cherries

In the boughs, red fruits abound,
Cherries chuckle with a sound.
Sweet laughter spills from berry lips,
As birds join in with playful quips.

Breezes tease, rustle and sway,
The fruits giggle in bright array.
Gathered crowds of buzzing bees,
Join the banter with gentle ease.

Each cherry sways, a merry dance,
Whispering secrets as they prance.
The moon peeks in, a jester too,
Illuminating all the hue.

With every bite, a burst of cheer,
Nature's jesters drawing near.
Chortles echo from tree to sky,
In this orchard where joy does fly!

Parables of the Pinecones

In a grove where pinecones scheme,
They chuckle in the sunlight's gleam.
Each roll and tumble brings a roar,
As squirrels plot to start a war.

With prickly jokes, they jest and tease,
How to drop on hapless knees.
A raindrop splashes, laughter swells,
They tell their tales, oh, how it dwells!

The wise old tree just shakes his trunk,
While whipping winds blow scents of funk.
"O pinecones, stop your clever pranks,
Or face the wrath of wandering janks!"

But pinecones wink, their spirits bright,
In every shadow, they find delight.
With each hilarious twist of fate,
Nature's jesters celebrate!

Secrets of the Sassy Saplings

Beneath the leaves, the saplings boast,
Of secrets hidden, they brag the most.
With roots that wriggle, and stems that sway,
They wink at passers with cheeky play.

A gust of wind brings giggles bold,
As wandering folk hear tales retold.
"Oh, did you see that dapper bug?"
"He danced on petals, what a smug tug!"

Unruly vines join in the jest,
Playing tricks, they never rest.
Each rustle brings a snort of glee,
In nature's court, the wise decree.

The bumblebee buzzes with a tune,
Singing praises to the afternoon.
Saplings shimmy and jiggle about,
Whispering secrets, without a doubt!

The Humor Hidden in the Hollies

In shady hollies, laughter blooms,
With daylight peeking through the glooms.
A napping owl with a twinkle's spark,
Dreams of mischief 'til it's dark.

The berries gossip, red and bright,
"Did you hear that laugh? What a sight!"
They bubble and chatter in merry cheer,
As cheeky squirrels scurry near.

Frogs in the pond croak a tune,
Making up rhymes to the light of the moon.
"Hop along now, you silly sprite!"
"Join the fun, it's pure delight!"

In the hollies, joy takes flight,
As whispers spark the starry night.
Each leaf a witness to the jest,
Where every creature is a guest!

Giggles among the Glades

In sunlit glades where secrets play,
The laughter of critters fills the day.
With prancing fawns and tadpoles that leap,
United in rhythm, their joy runs deep.

A hedgehog rolls with a snickered squeak,
While butterflies flutter with chatter unique.
"What do you call a frog in a suit?"
"A ribbit of class, he's quite the hoot!"

Each shadow dances, each whisper grins,
As raindrops giggle, and mischief begins.
The trees sway lightly, adding a beat,
To the symphony of life, oh so sweet!

So in these glades where chuckles flower,
Every creature finds their power.
In this playful haven under the sun,
Life's a jest, and we all just run!

The Irony of Ivy

In a leafy embrace, all jokes do reside,
A vine with a grin, where laughter can't hide.
Climbing up trees, it tickles the sky,
While squirrels roll their eyes, oh my, oh my!

Tangled in tales of absurdity's chase,
Ivy whispers secrets with a smirk on its face.
The branches all chuckle, the leaves join the fun,
A giggling garden, where everyone's spun.

In the shade of the bark, the giddiness grows,
The flora's got jokes that nobody knows.
With roots in the ground, it's a wild party scene,
Nature's own humor, forever unseen.

As the sun dips low, in a splash of deep green,
Ivy's punchlines linger, a soft, leafy sheen.
When laughter erupts, the twigs join the cheer,
In this fanciful patch, there's nothing to fear.

Joyous Jamboree in the Thicket

Under the canopy, where the shadows align,
A gathering's buzzing, a party divine.
The critters are dancing, with wiggles and shakes,
As the sun filters down, through the branches it makes.

With twirls and with whirls, the bushes do jig,
While rabbits on stilts attempt to do a gig.
The owls roll their eyes, the foxes all cheer,
In this wild thicket there's nothing to fear.

Berries in hats and mushrooms all dressed,
Are gossiping loudly with laughter, no rest.
A chorus of chuckles, a symphony bright,
In the heart of the thicket, all feels just right.

When daylight surrenders to twilight's embrace,
The party continues in this enchanted place.
Under stars' sparkling gaze, joy bursts at the seams,
In this merry assembly, we live out our dreams.

Amusing Acorns

Fallen and frolicking, the acorns convene,
With stories of mischief, they dance in between.
Drifting on breezes, they giggle and roll,
A comedy troupe with a nutty patrol.

They plot in the shadows, don hats made of leaves,
As squirrels act out their most comical thieves.
With every small tumble, the laughter's a blast,
Chasing each other, the joy unsurpassed.

A jester of nature, they crack jokes all day,
Creating a ruckus, come join in the play.
In humble surroundings, the fun reigns supreme,
Underneath mighty oaks, they weave a new dream.

When dusk casts its glow, their antics don't cease,
The acorns keep chuckling, spreading sweet peace.
In the heart of the forest, their laughter doth soar,
A nutty camaraderie, who could ask for more?

The Cheeky Clusters

Gathered together, in outrageous designs,
The clusters hold court, swapping playful lines.
With twigs for their stage and the sun as the light,
They banter and bicker from morning to night.

Beneath the broad leaves, the mischief is grand,
With shenanigans sprouting all over the land.
The chatter—oh golly!—it twists and it bends,
As nature's own clowns call out to old friends.

With berries aflutter, in flamboyant attire,
Their humor ignites, like a warm, crackling fire.
Twirling and spinning, through grass they do prance,
Unruly and merry, they lead us to dance.

As twilight approaches, they whisper and cheer,
Their laughter, our bond, oh how sweet to hear.
In the heart of the clusters, the joy's overflowing,
Together we bask in the whimsy they're showing.

Mischief in the Underbrush

In the thicket where shadows play,
A squirrel stole a nut today.
He scampers fast, a furry blur,
With a cheeky grin, he starts to purr.

Beneath the leaves, a rabbit pranks,
Jumping high on nearby banks.
He teases foxes, who chase in vain,
While laughing leaves swirl in the rain.

Chipmunks giggle, tucked in a hole,
Sharing tales, they stir the whole.
With beady eyes and twitchy tails,
They twirl the tales of nutty fails.

A dance of shadows, creatures share,
Misadventures in the open air.
With every rustle, laughter's near,
In the underbrush, joy's sincere.

Jests Beneath the Branches

Beneath the span of leafy crowns,
A parrot mocks the silly clowns.
With each caw, he cracks a joke,
As frogs below begin to croak.

A hedgehog rolls, a spiny ball,
He tumbles down, then starts to sprawl.
With giggles shared among the bloom,
They bring the light to grassy gloom.

Raccoons plot at the moonlit hour,
Debates on who found the best flower.
With winks and nudges, laughter swells,
In branches thick, the pleasure dwells.

So gather round, you merry crew,
There's fun to find in all we do.
Embrace the jests among the leaves,
Where every heart in jest believes.

Tales from the Toothy Thicket

In the thicket, where the shadows lie,
A wise old owl gives wisdom nigh.
He chuckles soft, so full of pride,
As chipmunks gather, eyes open wide.

A badger boasts of buried treats,
Claiming he hides the best of eats.
But in his den, he finds it bare,
With mice below who've stripped it there!

The rabbits craft a wild charade,
In clever tricks, their plans are laid.
A dance of paws, all leaps and bounds,
As laughter echoes round the grounds.

From leafy depths, a tale unfolds,
Of everything mischief boldly holds.
With toothy grins and cheerful cries,
The thicket thrives, where humor lies.

Banter of the Bark and Blossom

Under blossoms, jokes are spun,
The tree trunk cracks, "Oh, what fun!"
A bee buzzes with vibrant zest,
While flowers giggle, feeling blessed.

A crow remarks, "I'm quite the tease,
With shiny trinkets, I aim to please!"
But every time he makes a score,
The wind will swish, and he'll implore.

While petals flutter, gossip flows,
Of romps and run-ins, everyone knows.
With every bud, a story tall,
The bark gives life to laughter's call.

So come and join this lively band,
In nature's play, we take a stand.
With banter shared, no need for gloom,
Amidst the blooms, there's endless room.

The Nature of Nonsense

In a forest where jokes bloom bright,
Trees giggle softly in the moonlight.
The squirrels wear glasses, so wise,
While the frogs compose songs that surprise.

The mushrooms dance in their polka dots,
Making jokes that tether thoughts.
The breeze tells tales, both silly and sly,
As the leaves whisper secrets with a sigh.

Playful Pathways

On trails where the laughter grows,
A rabbit juggles carrots in rows.
The path twists and turns like a grin,
With surprises and giggles hidden within.

The owls hoot riddles from trees so tall,
While the hedgehogs play catch with a ball.
Every corner reveals a new jest,
In this land where humor's the guest.

Smiles and Shadows

In the glen where shadows meet,
Laughter echoes, a merry beat.
The shadows dance in silly ways,
As the sun sets and dims the rays.

The raccoon tells tales of daring feats,
While the spiders spin webs of treats.
Every chuckle brings smiles around,
In this world where joy is found.

The Jest of the Jungle

In a jungle where monkeys swing high,
A parrot squawks jokes as it flies by.
The vines tickle cheeks with a tease,
While the flowers giggle in the breeze.

The tigers wear stripes of comic flair,
With puns and gags filling the air.
In this land where laughter reigns,
Every moment is filled with playful gains.

The Woodland Winks

In shadows deep, a squirrel pranks,
The wise old owl just laughs and winks.
A bushy tail behind a tree,
Is that a joke or just a bee?

The mushrooms giggle in a row,
While ferns perform a show,
The hedgehog snickers, rolling near,
"Did I just hear a knock-knock here?"

The breeze whispers tales not shy,
As rabbits hop and dart nearby.
Each leaf a note in nature's song,
The forest hums where laughs belong.

So wander through this playful glade,
Where every creature shows its trade.
With smiles and chuckles, nature twirls,
In this land of giggling girls and whirls.

Banter by the Brook

By bubbling streams where thoughts collide,
The fish debate with lively pride.
"Who swims the fastest?" one remarks,
While ducks quack out their funny sparks.

A frog hops in, "I'll take the crown!"
With such a splash, he turns around.
But crickets chirp with sharp retorts,
"We're the stars of all the courts!"

The willows sway and join the fun,
As sunbeams dance and laughter run.
Each ripple in the water sings,
A jolly tune, as nature springs.

So lean in close and hear the jest,
Where babbling brooks are at their best.
With laughter echoing through the air,
Join in and relish without a care.

The Laughing Logger

In timberland, a logger grins,
With tales of trees and gentle spins.
"Cut down this one? A joke, it seems,
For it has far too many dreams!"

He talks to trunks with jest so bright,
"Don't worry, friend, you're safe tonight!"
While chips fly high, he laughs aloud,
Nature's whispers grow so proud.

"Logs can't talk, but they can shout,
With every ring, their tales come out."
With humor sharp as a fresh saw's bite,
He shares a grin with the starry night.

So wander where the laughter flows,
Amongst the trees where good cheer grows.
For in this place of playful quirk,
You'll find the joy, the heartfelt smirk.

Oak and Aha!

Beneath the oak so grand and stout,
The critters dance, they twist about.
"Why did the acorn sit and stare?"
"Because it dreamed to grow up there!"

The chipmunks chuckle in a row,
As shadows play, put on a show.
"Did you hear the pine tree's song?"
"It said, 'I've been here all along!'"

The mossy floor holds secrets deep,
Where laughter stirs from peaceful sleep.
As squirrels tease, they squeal with glee,
"A nutty world, so fun to be!"

So gather round, let joy set free,
In forests rich with jolly glee.
For every leaf holds a little cheer,
In the heart of woods, we all draw near.

The Whimsy of Willows

In a glade where laughter rings,
Willows sway with playful swings.
A raccoon dons a feathered hat,
Claiming he's the king of chat.

Buzzing bees throw dance galas,
While frogs croak out sweet balladas.
Squirrels jest with acorn hats,
Charming every wanderer that chats.

The sunlight twinkles, winks with glee,
As flowers join in harmony.
A breeze carries a chuckling sigh,
Nature's jesters all nearby.

Underneath the shade so grand,
Friendship blossoms hand in hand.
Each curve of branch and twisted vine,
Reminds us all of laughter's line.

The Folly of Forest Friends

In the heart where hedgehogs roam,
Foxes laugh, they feel at home.
A rabbit spins a merry tale,
Of how he danced and made a sail.

Owls with glasses write down notes,
About the squirrels' acrobatic boats.
The deer play hide and seek by noon,
While crickets strum a jovial tune.

Badgers paint with berry stains,
Creating art on summer's lanes.
Chipmunks chatter, full of fun,
Competing who can make a pun.

Underneath a bright blue sky,
Laughter echoes, oh so spry.
From every nook and shady bend,
The forest finds its joy, my friend.

Revels in the Reeds

Where tall and merry grasses dance,
Mice in tuxedos take their chance.
With pockets filled with seeds of cheer,
They throw a bash, bring all friends near.

The dragonflies spin drops of light,
While frogs compete in leaps of height.
A party breaks at dawn's first glow,
As fireflies put on a dazzling show.

Cattails bob like party hats,
As turtles join in with their spats.
They wink and wave with such delight,
In nature's gathering, a true sight.

As stars twinkle in the deep blue,
The night teems with laughter anew.
In the reeds where joy entreats,
The revelry never retreats.

Bouncing Between the Branches

In the treetops, fun takes flight,
Kites played tag with pure delight.
Monkeys swing with cheeky grins,
Crafting jests as the laughter spins.

A parrot shouts, 'What's that you say?'
As squirrels plot their grand ballet.
Branches bend with playful hugs,
While raccoons share their hidden mugs.

The nightingale croons his silly tune,
Injecting joy beneath the moon.
Amidst the leaves, the whispers rise,
Of antics shared and fleeting sighs.

Every tree a stage so fine,
Where nature's jesters intertwine.
Bouncing high, they meet with grace,
In the woodland's merry embrace.

Laughter at the Underbrush

A squirrel in a top hat danced,
Chasing shadows with a glance.
The mushrooms giggled, green and round,
As the breeze hummed a silly sound.

A rabbit tossed a leafy crown,
While the bees wore coats of brown.
Each twig was twirled, a jolly wand,
As laughter echoed through the pond.

A turtle slipped in polka dots,
Played hopscotch over tangled knots.
He winked at snails with shells so bright,
And crafted jokes with all his might.

So join the fun, bring mirth anew,
In this realm where giggles grew.
Each rustle holds a hearty laugh,
In the underbrush, let joy be your path.

Jovial Journey through the Canopy

A parrot dressed in rainbow flair,
Sipped juice from a balmy pear.
Branches danced in bright array,
As monkeys swung in grand ballet.

The owls wore specs, a learned bunch,
Debating fruit for their next lunch.
With whispered jokes and playful cheers,
They sprinkled laughter through the years.

Swaying vines held tales of fun,
While sunbeams played, a golden run.
Bouncing berries shared their lore,
Each bounce a giggle, never a bore.

Up above where feathers blend,
Nature laughs, around each bend.
A tapestry of joy unfurled,
In this delightful, greenscape world.

The Frolicsome Forest Floor

Beneath the ferns, a dance began,
With squirrels joining, hand in hand.
The pebbles chuckled, rolling round,
As merry critters gathered 'round.

Acorns spun like tiny tops,
The snickering of a toad that pops.
A hedgehog wiggled, full of cheer,
He made a joke that all could hear.

With every rustle and tiny sound,
The forest floor was joy unbound.
Bouncing twigs and leafy cheers,
Grew with the chatter over the years.

So tiptoe softly, join the spree,
With laughter shared as wild and free.
The frolicsome floor holds jests galore,
An invitation to explore.

Droll Delights of the Dawn

As dawn broke with a yawn so wide,
The critters roused, their laughter tied.
Morning glimmers sparkled bright,
Tickled leaves began to light.

A fox displayed his latest trick,
He juggled nuts and danced so quick.
The crickets chirped with spicy glee,
Creating tunes for all to see.

The flowers chuckled, petals swayed,
In a sunlit show, they would parade.
With every giggle, the day was spun,
In droll delights, the morning run.

So gather 'round, let laughter chime,
In morning's glow, it's jesting time.
The forest hums with pure delight,
As dawn awakens, everything feels right.

www.ingramcontent.com/pod-product-compliance
Lightning Source LLC
Chambersburg PA
CBHW051647160426
43209CB00004B/829